ISCA

- Exeter Moments -

ISCA

- Exeter Moments -

WILLIAM OXLEY

Photography by
BARRY DAVIDSON

Ember Press
2013

Acknowledgement is due to the following where some of these poems first appeared: *Equinox; www.falconpress.com; The Interpreter's House, Littoral, Only Connect Anthology* (Cinnamon Press)*; Three Candles (USA),* and *High on the Downs: a Festschrift for Harry Guest,* ed. Tony Lopz, Shearsman Books 2012. Thanks are also due to members of the staff of Exeter Cathedral in permitting Barry Davidson's photographs of the interior to be reproduced.

A c-i-p record for this title is available from the British Library

ISBN 978 - 1 - 873161 - 37 - 1

Published by
Ember Press
6 The Mount
Higher Furzeham
Brixham, Devon
TQ5 8QY UK

INTRODUCTION

Poems should always speak for themselves. As, probably, should all books. But it is a well-known fact that readers of most books – perhaps novels are the exception – are pleased to encounter a welcome mat at the book's entrance. Not as something for critics to wipe their feet on, but as supplying some information as to the genesis of the work itself.

The author of *Isca*, having lived in South Devon for many years, has had occasion to visit Exeter from time to time. His introduction to the city itself came about as a result of the business of poetry. Having been drawn to Exeter as a consequence of meeting a number of fellow poets there, it was inevitable that a response to the place would be induced by the Muse from time to time. Such 'responses' resulted in poems that were either written on the spot, 'the spontaneous overflow of powerful feeling' – in the Cathedral grounds or The Well House pub, for examples – or back at home in his study in Torbay as, 'emotion recollected in tranquillity': to borrow two of Wordsworth's best known critical phrases.

So, in a sense, these poems over time built themselves into the current collection by virtue of place. However, it was felt that given the fact that all the poems are, in some degree, Exeter-City-centred; or, in the case of those about the city's environs incline, like any view of Exeter itself from the countryside, towards, not away from, its cathedral, it would be helpful for any readers to have some photographic accompaniment. This last idea having been accomplished, the poet hopes that the visual has helped considerably towards the final shaping of the verbal. And that this partnership will add much to any reader's enjoyment of the book.

Finally, I would like to thank Barry Davidson, the photographer, my daughter Elizabeth, my wife Patricia and Danielle Hope, all of whom contributed thoughtful input into the making and shaping of the book. Also, to the late David Beugger who accompanied me on many trips to Exeter and who shared many of the moments in this book.

William Oxley
Brixham
July 2012

VOICES

A few yards from Hooker's statue
and the angel on the faded façade
of God's big house, still
missing a finger, hand over heart.

Hand over heart for the beat
of life. All around, too,
the noise of life: students on the
wet cathedral green who do not care,

and in the pub that calls itself
a tavern, voices, voices, voices
and the scrape of chairs on faded
floor. Voices like the invisible

leaves of autumn. Voices, not
angelic, that speak in silence
straight to the heart. No, when
mystery speaks it is mystery no more.

Voices that hang about in the head
and mingle with the silent...
these are what I experience
these are possibly all we have.

This old place marinaded
in wood and wine, beer and the blackness
of time. This place of personal shadows,
Rupert, Phil, Dave, and Tony the one
really dead: the others gone
or going from my life, now shadows
and friendship's shadows
whom I lament, autumn keening for summer.
Phil (with Mary then, the fine-figured
widow), Phil the entertainer, the
real performance poet, no clown
how he could clown! Dave, the budding
arts' apparatchik, his gaze bluff
as a beard can make it, that
seeming openness of the diplomat keeping
much close to his chest.

REMEMBERING THE WHITE HART, SOUTH SREET.

        Tony, another failed
actor really, poetry publisher but,
in reality, more a fan of Elvis's
than Eluard, of Madonna than Marvell –
tobacco's cancer sticks got him.
Now they are all gone from this
ancient city, trailing their clouds of unglory
behind. I still see their pleasing shades,
personalities of yesterday, somehow freed
for me of aspirations and failure,
the pains and contentments of life, gone
now from this pub, this place, lost
players of life who in my prayers
of friendship I recall, talk with still.
But Rupert – poet, painter, publisher –
most missed. Autumn keening for summer.

GEORGE'S MEETING HOUSE, EXETER

I can see them all now, they who
knew they were close to God –
or believed so. Lives of hardship and plod
through long pastures of pain. Any way
would do in their day, for all ways led
to Zion. Often their children starved,
most ailments were believed cured by being 'bled'.
A great day was when a cow calved
or another child was born: the least thing
or the greatest a cause for celebration.
Half-mired in suffering they could still sing,
live out each day with resignation –
like only artists now, waiting inspiration
for that pouring light out of oblivion.

IN AN EXETER CHURCH

The throb of traffic contests the grubby silence
Of St. Olav's church, disturbs the presence
Round a man. The day outside roars with heat.
Christ alone is calm and cool upon a neat
Victorian cross. Virgin and child, too, on a triptych
Ornate, baroque, well-meant and rich:
A flash of blue, red and gold that fills
Emptiness like a fugue of flowers thrills
Some corner of a garden. Here wrong and right
Have masqueraded in hope of finding that white
Tremendous gleam way past any sun, far,
Farther than the remotest, vaguest star.
And who can say it has not, has not
Sometimes shone: love's spark, that infinite dot.

ECCLESIASTICAL POLITY

His statue is thoughtful, bookish, grey
                            but not grave
in the green cathedral close. Beneath the
                            great gaze
of holy history, Richard Hooker ponders
                            genially
as an August evening turns the massed
                            frontage
to a cliff of shine. And the saints
                            look down
upon the man who justified the ways
                            of Anglicanism
to God, and began the emancipation
                            of prose,
English prose – shining the light of faith
                            into every
corner of its dark and clotted syntax. Hooker
                            for love,
and Swift for hate, taught
                            the secret
of a living style that is clarity of mind
joined with the subtleties of God.

THE   WELL

A few yards from here Exeter's cathedral green
A few yards from here the Roman garrison's baths
A few yards from here the first ever English hotel

HOUSE

A few yards from here Drake's local pub
A few yards from here so much history
But fewer yards still the whole human mystery

THE SHADOW OF THE WIND

Even the winds of June will search you out
Even those faults that are normal shall show
Like the sorrows and illnesses each of us would flee.

But there is another wind than winds of the world
It is the wind of shadows that you may feel –
A wind that blows beautiful and silent
The wind of stars that fill the emptiest space.

It is the last wind of all, wind of shadows
And no direction – in the first few hours of life
It wraps like an invisible shawl each baby –
Yes, the last wind, and the first, like hope
And you know, of course, it is the wind of love.

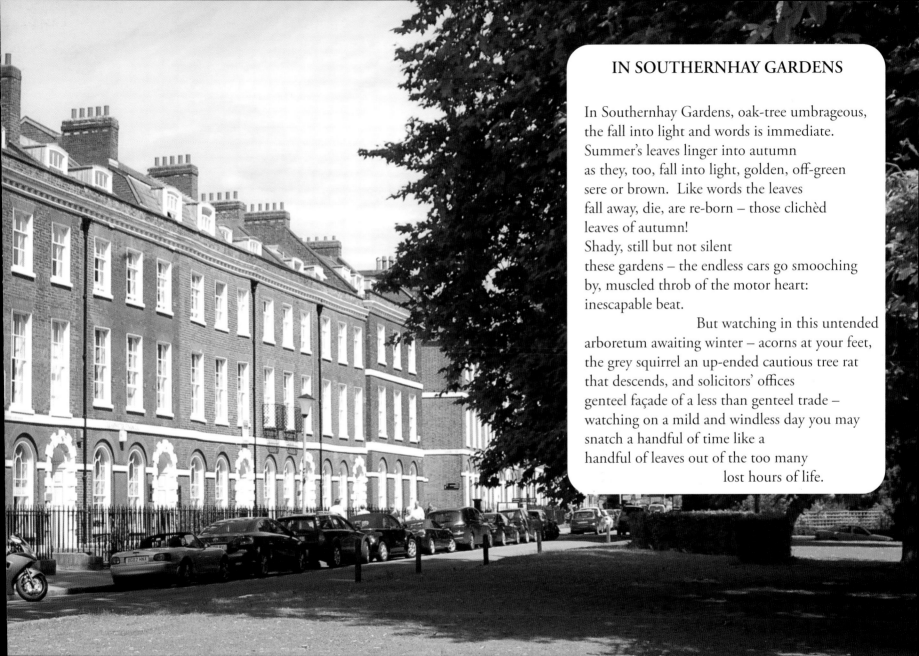

IN SOUTHERNHAY GARDENS

In Southernhay Gardens, oak-tree umbrageous,
the fall into light and words is immediate.
Summer's leaves linger into autumn
as they, too, fall into light, golden, off-green
sere or brown. Like words the leaves
fall away, die, are re-born – those clichèd
leaves of autumn!
Shady, still but not silent
these gardens – the endless cars go smooching
by, muscled throb of the motor heart:
inescapable beat.

                    But watching in this untended
arboretum awaiting winter – acorns at your feet,
the grey squirrel an up-ended cautious tree rat
that descends, and solicitors' offices
genteel façade of a less than genteel trade –
watching on a mild and windless day you may
snatch a handful of time like a
handful of leaves out of the too many
                        lost hours of life.

ROUGEMONT DREAM

(Rougemont Castle, Exeter)

In the park
the winos cuddle bottles
growl and glare at passers-by.
They dream in order not to die.

Mounds and walls
where *knyghts did clash*
and nights are raven-high.

It's hearing history
we are. Dead time sleeps here,
tells a story

how we became.
Lords and ladies in procession
dazzling night-sights:

brilliant figures,
though they stink as much
as any following rabble.

Mound, walls and dead wells,
stonework that reaches skyward:
drawbridges draw us back

to dreams of fear, reason
ruined by sight of ruins.
We are all asleep

until dreams come. In the park
the winos cuddle bottles.
They dream in order not to die.

Lacking vision when awake –
imagination feeds on dark –
we dream in order we may live.

19

FLOOD PLAIN

1

Each inter-city express
slithers across it like a serpent,

on wind stressed ponds
alabaster swans circulate.

Cows browse and defecate.
A green sponge wedged between

tree-frayed hills and a glaring
estuary that is mud-rimmed.

Mallards, herons, gulls, and cattle-
tormenting crows populate

this open-faced, sun-sucked wetland.
Days stack up here and

their supply has no end. Unlike
in cities there is no bitterness

but hope, the sweet taste of light,
openness, whatever ...

2

And it was hope
helped men grope
their way through slime
of time
to better vision
of civilization;
and right next
the River Exe
build a canal
to channel
and slow
river's overflow.

Begun in Tudor days
it found its way
eventually

to muddy estuary
and into history
as first ever waterway
to have pound locks:
gates to block
not slow but stop,
as weir cannot,
flow or flood.
for human good.

3

Upon this open land fringed by water
the tall sun shines a timeless eye

lighting low-hedged fields and sunken
                                    lanes
dark ponds where cattle congregate –

in such a scene there is a poetry, like
the slow coursing of history and dream.

AS GOOD A PLACE AS ANY

(i.m. Ken Smith)

It is winter's carpet
rolling into greeting-card spring.
Clouds cling
to stanza lines of oak and ash.

A man I knew
walked here years ago
letting the mind slow,
to unwind its twisty, barbed wires

of responsibility. Between
the gleam of canal and river
a lemon sliver
of sun. Goal-posts and white
      markings

but no screams of teams.
Flat as a playing field is death.
His lost breath
I still see like a roll-up's smoke.

He's dead now
the man I once knew. For him,
even then,
the shadows were moving in.

But he still walks by my mind,
and making a poem talks
as he walks.
And a playing field's as good a place
      as any.

DRAKE'S PUB

The eternal lightning flashes on him
and he's in Drake's wooden pub.
Old, medieval and dim;
wine-red, beer-brown, good grub.

The same flashed on another poet too.
A sad one. A good one. Smith
once scribbled in this bacchic purlieu.
Till he decided to give it a miss

and went AWOL to another life
and different wife. Same muse though.
Out the corner of a window's eye, leaf
on leaf leaps in autumn's slow

dance. Winter's indifferent rain
is coming. And weakly leaking suns
that make the great cathedral glow again:
glow as time on its stones runs and runs.

The drinker his eyes full of delight
in dark light, lingers with
his northern singer, that bright
fox-fleeing revenant Ken Smith

who made a poem in there.
For a poet takes to heart history's
long confused tale told everywhere.
Is a sleuth button-holing mysteries.

CLONE CITY COMPLAINT

*Exeter, the city of Augustus' 2nd Legion, was described in
a recent report as 'Britain's most cloned city'.*
— BBC Radio News, 6.6.05

I was Augustus' city, a primitive place
Finally freed from a savage race,

And was built in the latest Roman style:
A development that took quite a while.

First erected was my formidable wall
As protection for villa and market stall,

Then baths and barracks and temples too
Till just about everything was built anew.

Proud on my hill I grew the civilized way
And was only sad when Rome had had its day.

Not, of course, when the legion departed
But two centuries after they'd got me started

When barbarians sailed up the River Exe
To destroy my buildings, leave smoking wrecks.

Then since Saxon and Norman it's been all change.
But even when prosperity's about it's strange

How hurtful folk are and discontented
Because all my shops have now been rented

By Primark and Waterstones, Marks and Boots —
In fact all the usual retail offshoots

That other cities and other towns possess.
But it's me that gets called 'a uniform mess'!

THE UNKNOWN SCULPTOR

Statues in bas relief, kings, apostles –
wonderful weathered faces of the dead
up the high front, the cathedral cliff
that the sea of time has battered.
How in the secular now so many yearn
to feel the draught of even one angel's wing!
The ease of want in the age of money,
sex's last mystery no longer satisfying.

Does the divine image still live in these stones?
The wonderful weathered faces of the dead.
Hold your breath, visitor, and consider
there's an art here by which you might be led.
Came to meet a friend in the legion's city, Isca,
that is now known as plain Exeter –
his birth city it was I wanted to discover.
But what I found again was work of the unknown sculptor.

SOMETHING MISSING

Hand on heart an angel with little finger missing
on the Cathedral's façade. Then hear a choir singing
and the longing begins again, all over again,
for a life that is both now and then.

BOOKS ANCIENT AND MODERN

Trundled the old Exeter Book to
the publication party for a new one.
Dean of the Cathedral brought it.
With buttersmooth face openly
proffered the huge bound book,
preponderant tome in any room.
'Alas, only a copy – the original's
under lock-and-key, insured
for millions of pounds,'
said he, giving his best facsimile smile.

The first edition to end all first editions!
The premier collection of poetry
in the English tongue when still Anglo-Saxon.
'The Wanderer's book', 'Widsith and Deor',
'The Seafarer', 'The Ruin' and
those strange riddles, posers
to be done afresh for the 3rd Millennium.

The old Exeter Book, stained
by marshy dankness, charred by
fire of forgotten skirmishes,
lovingly fondled by cryptic
scholars and scribes, scraped by
indifferent priests, now a
bone-smelling book laid before poets,
new makers of new riddles –
wine-bright faces at a wine-bright party
in a still haunted city.

The Old Exeter Book c.10th century

The New Exeter Book of Riddles, AD 2000

27

THE BLOSSOMING

A poem's essential condition for making:
it is like writing on the sky.
A poem has to make facts blossom:
like the fish-and-chip shop that serves Mars bars in batter
in the queer old city of Exeter –
its park gates ornate with a coat-of-arms
Semper Fidelis, two winged horses rampant,
and knightly figure with castle on escutcheon;
or stone statue of man and hound, its legend
'The Deer Stalker' (fine body but face too Greek);
and noises: aircraft, pneumatic drill, vehicles,
human voices and occasional rattle of birdsong;
in Northernhay Gardens squashed, crumpled
decomposing leaves of, mostly, stripped trees:
their branches, their figures, their leaves
like captured notes of musical imagination,
dockets in autumn's blue air suspended ...
yes, writing a poem, is making facts blossom.

RESOLUTION IN EXETER PUB

A businessman reading newspapers,
a semi-invalid puffing in his beer,
piped black musak moaning here
and me into another living year.

Somehow must make it all cohere,
not slip away like used-up love,
a dye dispersing in water.
Needed: a great imaginative shove

so as to enter all those dreams –
the long splendours we see
day by day but seldom reach:
inches away, their star-gilded reality.

THE LABURNUM TREE

He stands there on a kerbside
ignoring the animal cars' cries –
a yellow tree of laburnum is
beauty to his eyes

A man threads the best days
of life with too many sorrows –
hearing, brown and busy,
the beautiful sparrows

flitting from perch to perch, motes
behind the yellow tears of
the tree. Birds do not know
how much they love.

Nor that this tree is a poison tree.
He knows within his breast
is a terrible beauty that
allows no living rest.

Soft and sweet, soft and sweet
the moments pass
for a man transfixed in sight
who only wants to bless.

LOOKING AT YOU AGAIN, RICHARD HOOKER

Well, Hooker, here I am looking at your stone
                              effigy again.
How remote you look in history's anglicized
                              rain.
In today's cold winter weather you are
                              plain
as your prose. White, mildew-scabbed but sculpted
                              perfectly,
your pilgrim's almost-Chinese hat
                              firmly
on your stone head, your long prophetic face
                              blindly-kindly
staring into everlasting futures of holiness
                              not compatible
with secular futures where musak of pubs
hymn the endgame being played out in cyber clubs
and other marvellous innovations of a dying world
that may, Richard Hooker, soon join you in your
                              stone past:
all this planet once green now being
                              greenly gassed.

NIETZSCHE IN EXETER

'Many lands saw Zarathustra,
and many peoples'
          from *'The Thousand & One Goals'* – Nietzsche.

The tender sweep of parkland
moulded by a great hand
between St. David's station
and the Exeter river basin,

cut by a scimitar of water.
Alongside the canal a walker
wrapped in his mind, a Nietzsche
a thinker, a Cathedral preacher –

catches a reflection
of himself. Sudden salvation
of seeing through oneself
the moment of inestimable truth.

All his being danced, wise
with celebration and praise,
like a dancer in verse,
he danced to the end of the universe.

ENCOUNTERING POSTMODERNISM
IN REALITY

'If he'd got his eyes open
his mouth would be down a level ...'
Words in an evening bar somehow
recalled how we'd been walking
the water ruler of a straight canal
that passes under a fly-over's
mighty concrete.
        And there,
at that exact spot, with no
visible access to the towpath
but our four-mile tramp from Starcross,
two young women – models for
Vogue – seated on a stone slab
illustrating virtual reality
in pure colour photography:
high heels, make-up, mobiles,
dresses bright as flowers –
and no way they could be there
'miles from anywhere',
but they were, they were.

AT THE DOUBLE LOCKS' PUB

Perfected by pouring sun the canal
stretched a golden way to distant estuary
and vibrant sea. All was autumnal.
Then 'the heart's affections' sucked out
'the truth of imagination'
by The Double Locks' pub where duck and coot,

day and air, were languid and musical.
How could hatred ever be possible?
Is not the world always miraculous, as gentle

sun on a green plain in special light,
like then? Secular or not, a simplicity
is everywhere if men would see straight,

for Chris and Penny

hear the speech of wind, grass-mutter,
note artistic flow and form of cloud,
and above a pub's hubbub hear drip of water,

the slow secretion of a love that is sea-vast,
unchangeable as past or future.
A voice pleads, Look, look, be blest!
At this pub by uncompetitive waters
there was, that day, much talk
of terrorism and far-off slaughter

and the contests of peace were not heard
as, perfected by pouring sun, the canal
stretched its shining to the estuary
and even golden became a golden melancholy.

OFF THE HOOK
(St. Stephen's Church, Exeter)

Voices in the cupola
rise and echo
unwind as slow
as petals of faith
falling to dry silence,
the sinner's self-gutting
prayer. Quitting

the gilded precincts
 – not imaged by Old Masters
but by humbler artisans –
is to re-enter the welcome
sprawl of life

where street musicians play
safe, money counts,
and you are somehow
off the hook for now.

LIVING HISTORY FESTIVAL, NORTHERNHAY GARDENS

Narrow uplifted park viewing
the spread of Exeter's
clear rooftops and clutter,
and green hills foaming
under restive skies. Historic skies.

A day of living history in that
shabby-cornered park,
its gross monument reptilian
moulded of Victorian metal.
A day of living history displacing
winos, druggies, dogs. A day too
for kids on a yellow Sabbath.

Two legionaries by the gates, armoured
informants, ready to recreate the darkbright
past for free. Bought their own outfits too:
'A centurion's gear's above two grand'.
On a red banner these words:
        AUG II LEG.
The 2nd Augustan Legion, 40 years
in situ before it left:
        AURA AUGUSTA PACIS ISCA.

In the shadow of Rougemont's redstone
(its layered wall Roman/Saxon/Norman)
were stalls of surpassing interest
like the medieval music man, sweetly
proud of his many instruments on display
who played on the lyre a soft-sounding tune,
Pindaric, he said, culled from some Attic stone.
And at the nearby scriptorum we tried a stylus –
Virgil wrote verse on wax. Difficult,
like tracing on soft caramel.
Next, a tournament. Heavy armoured thugs,
knights in murderous conflict but with
blunted swords ... 'More knights died
of dehydration than wounds then' – so when
a warrior rested, his fair damsel
in undistress brought bottled water,
before returning to the helmet-dinting fray:
'as true a ding-dong as you'll get today!'

Archery, rope-making, singing of madrigals,
pageantry, all the fun of a Bartholomew Fair,
very much a Chaucerian day, or Langland's
faire felde ful of folke. Until, of course,
it rained, and rain had the last word:
England's history is a wet history,
        and a bloody one.

READING THE EMBROIDERED RONDELS

(Exeter Cathedral)

Wind sighing, howling through the great door
of the Cathedral, the spirit and physical law
are one – 'in Christ is all made alive' –
I twist the words out of a poet's love
not disbelief, as from these embroidered seats
where a multi-coloured, many-sided history greets
the eye I copy dead snippets of Exeter:
'Battle of Pinhoe 658AD. Anglo-Saxons take Exeter,
live peaceably with the British ...'
Peace, always threatened, peace something we always wish
to have, though Lawrence said it meant 'Universal death',
'peace' the word whispered under every breath,
and when it came in that far-off time at Pinhoe
King Cenwealh built an abbey we now know
was called after St Mary and St Peter –

original of this Cathedral, stone palace of God.
Then, as this same love-worked rondel said,
'Alfred came to Exeter and made a truce'
(keeping historic faith its embroidered use)
'with the Danes one year after they had come
and in August 877AD. the surly pagans were gone'.
Only to return long after the great King was dead
until, in AD.1001, things once more came to a head
at the second Battle of Pinhoe when 'King Ethelred
defeated the Danes', promising a Saxon mark 'outlaid
each year for the local priest', and it's still paid.
– And so in this strange inner-outer wind
that stirs every soul however blind,
and blows high as roof-boss, low as ground,
the living Christ of history can be found.

BREAKFAST AT THE BASIN
(Exeter Quay)

The cobbled waterfront
medieval surface like watered boils
but a sweet, healthy sun
sweeps majestic rays
across miles of still water
long as memory. Yes,
memory, memory, memories
of this Anglo-Roman-Norman city.

And if you love it like me
you, too, shall inherit memory
that many strata'd encirclement
like Exeter's time-trapped wall:
memory of things you cannot know
as that memory, a once-time
I drew a finger over stone,
cathedral stone, and the yellow dust
that fell, fell from an angel's wing
a sort of dry dead sunlight
the colour of the invisible.

And this harboured water
with its gossiping crowd of ducks and swans
is really a welcome pool of infinity
the source of life and idea.

41

PANCAKES AND WORDS, EXETER

Gandy Street
once had an eatery
called The Crêperie.

Gandy Street where
Thomas Bodley dwelt
before he went to Oxford,

but not where he –
founder of the famous library –
ate in Gandy Street.

But some of us –
if the food cost much
and drinking more –
still found its tables,

boards and gourmet air
to our taste, for
The Crêperie was the place
to eat best pancakes –
and, now and then, our words.

EYES IN STONE

(Exeter Cathedral)

The fan-vaulted roof,
the windows letting in light,
    vast image of truth
the eternal eternally right

    and in every last part
echoes of human voices,
    and the silence vast
in which something rejoices.

    It is transformed stone
that the heart amazes:
    cold, yes, and alone
but how like the living it gazes

    back at its makers, men.
In stones as in flowers
    are eyes that shine when
love rains its sudden showers.

43

THE IRON BRIDGE

Above the iron bridge
day faded into grey

A figure passed by
who or why was hard to say

(A pub called The Exchange
exchanged memories.)

I who am not I
but also him and her, try

to recall the dead now gone
(like Sir Jim for one)

and the still living who don't
now gather there, can't or won't.

Being of course will last
but not without a past:

'Before Abraham I was',
After each moment a new I am.

So today we praise
those good drinking days

in that pub by the bridge
(where day still fades into grey)

where another waved and walked
above as we talked –

and were not ourselves there
for a while in Exeter.

ISCA JOTTINGS

The Exeter Basin: still quays, mirrors of water, swans in a heatwave. A duck's feather of cloud reflected. Mango's bistro, outdoor tables, a place for breakfast.

Southernhay Gardens: Commerce and the Law among oaks and sycamores. A whiff of cigarette, fragments of drifting scent, summer lounges about like a hot woman.

'What do you best remember of Exeter?'
'Rupert and the Romans.'
I remember the regular blocks of volcanic trap, Roman stratum of the city's walls. Rupert, poet, painter, publisher – he once published me. 'I liked his sense of humour and I've always been fascinated by the Romans.' Isca Romanorum.

A small grey van parked. Large letters on its side: JC MILTON (Electrical Contractors) It reminds of my years of meditation in Moorfields, London's Barbican. John Milton is buried there in St. Giles Cripplegate. And now that all my friends have left, Isca too is another of my cities of the past.

Southernhay Gardens where the trees offer truly umbrageous shade. One thought preoccupies: Is the past a woman?

Barnfield Theatre. O how have I never found this before? A deliciously shabby place. Small Costa Coffee cafe and box-office on ground floor. One table outside shaded by awning. The place redolent of Victorian English eccentricity. A professional theatre with amateur air...like Exeter among cities.

Northernhay Gardens' notice board: 'Exeter's history stretches back for nearly 2000 years. The first major settlement was by the Roman 2nd Augustan legion in 55AD. A legionary fortress established overlooking the lowest crossing point of the River Exe and defended by the steep sided Longbrook Valley and the River Exe itself. This first fortification was known as Isca...'

The Albert Memorial Museum. Where the Romans now dwell.

Northernhay Gardens. Yards from the war memorial to those who gave their lives in the Great War ('Their name shall live for evermore') a group of the Unwashed Young, one with guitar, 'drugged up to the eyeballs', drunk, a red-faced woman screeching imprecations, expletives. ('They died in mud that scum should be free.').

The Phoenix Arts Centre. Colourful place, coloured by memories: *In the present a dark-haired young woman 'waiting for inspiration', pen poised over yellow paper. In the past 'You had one of your 60th birthdays in this place.' And* The New Exeter Book of Riddles *was launched here by Enitharmon Press to celebrate the new millennium. Not far away, in the cramped and dusty cathedral library the old* Exeter Book: *first book of poetry in English (O.E.)*

Faint smell of tobacco smoke in bar today; breeze through an open window; young love wrestling on leather sofa; woman still awaiting inspiration. All art reflects the search for meaning. And wisdom? The meaning of God.

Poetry now? How the space allotted to it in Exeter's book shops has shrunk. Waterstones, etc. Is it a surprise? *New Generation Poets, Next Generation Poets* but no *No Generation Poets*? Media-promotions. The Muse, media-bathing, become an old kipper in the sun.

Poetry is the ceaseless search for new expression. It is Isca constantly renewing itself as Exeter.

My Exeter. Who are the vanished? Rupert, Sue, Louise, Mary, the two Anns (Born & Gray), Alexis L., James H., Phil B., Dave W. and others ... the Already Forgotten. Am I destined to move on? Am I man or city?

The People of Exeter: such faces, such profiles, such expressions! Rembrandt would have loved you.

Bars: The Exchange, The Well House, The Phoenix, Sir Francis Drake's The Ship. Wine and friendship. Wine and solitude (anonymity better term?) Wine and inspiration.

Facts: The Royal Clarence, Exeter, England's first-ever hotel.

Parliament Street, Exeter, the world's narrowest street.

The popularity of translating *The Commedia* testifies to the Age of Revenge. The popularity of translating today testifies to the Age of Uninspiration.

Like I didn't say, but do now: Exeter *pour moi c'est une cité des pensées.*

Exeter Cathedral, all the pictures:

'The Nativity', Gherrard delle Notti, 1590-1656

'Icon of Christ Pantocrator', copy 14th C. Greek

'The Virgin of the Rocks', copy Da Vinci, 1452-1519

'Madonna della Sedra', after Raphael, 1483-1520.

He took off his hat in Exeter Cathedral as a mark of respect and somehow lost it. Better his hat than his head. A poet can make almost something out of nothing: only God can go the whole hog.

The First Coming gave hope of the Second Coming. The sort of thought one has in a great cathedral. Is it a voice out of silence gives such notions? The silent voice of Truth? Or what?

2006 in the above-mentioned arts centre: a standard glass of red wine £2.50; a large £3.60. 2006: entrance to the Cathedral, the House of God: free. 2010 entrance to the Cathedral: £5.00.

Words are the material of poetry: words, process and structure. Exeter Cathedral is a great poem built of one word: exaltation.

Last words: friends, like this city you wrote yourselves into my life, then left. 'People move on' – one of the saddest phrases in the language of feeling. The soul of a city is made changeless by change.

Isca to Exeter via eternity.